THE ELEMENTS

Cobalt

Susan Watt

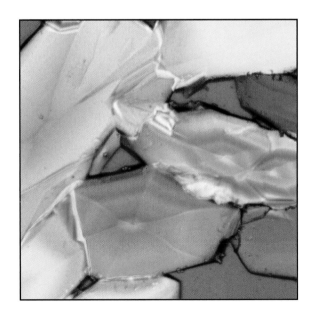

Marshall Cavendish
Benchmark

New York

Marshall Cavendish Benchmark
99 White Plains Road
Tarrytown, New York 10591

www.marshallcavendish.us

© Marshall Cavendish Corporation, 2007

Library of Congress Cataloging-in-Publication Data

Watt, Susan, 1958–
Cobalt / Susan Watt.
p.   cm. — (The elements)
Includes index.
ISBN-13: 978-0-7614-2200-6
ISBN-10: 0-7614-2200-5
Cobalt—Juvenile literature. 2. Chemical elements—Juvenile literature. I. Title. II.
Elements (Marshall Cavendish Benchmark)
QD181.C6W38 2007
546'.623—dc22

2005055303

1 6 5 4 3 2

Printed in Malaysia

Picture credits
Front cover: PBase
Back cover: Atlantic Ablestock

Ablestock: 22
Stan Celestian: 10
Corbis: Lester V. Bergman 27, Liz Gilbert 12, Roger Ressmeyer 5
Corbis Royalty Free: 20
Digital Vision: 19
Johnson & Johnson: 3, 25
PBase: 4
Photos.com: 1, 11, 23, 24, 26
Science & Society: Science Museum 6
Science Photo Library: 30, Andrew Lambert Photography 7, 17, Jerry Mason 15

Series created by The Brown Reference Group plc.
Designed by Sarah Williams
www.brownreference.com

Contents

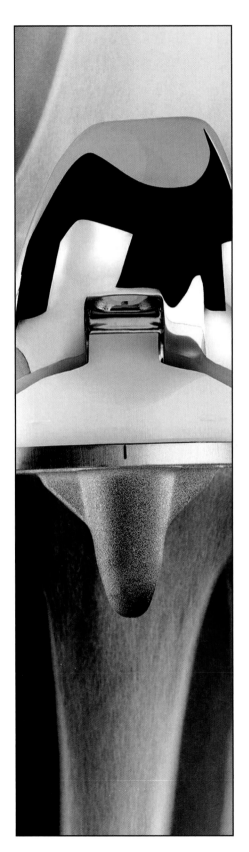

What is cobalt?

Cobalt is one of life's essential elements, at least for humans and animals. We could not survive without it. Like twenty-six other elements, cobalt is a necessary part of our bodies. Cobalt is the central atom in each molecule of vitamin B_{12}, which is an important substance that we get in our food. Vitamin B_{12} helps the body make blood.

Cobalt has plenty of other uses. The most familiar use is probably as a coloring material for glass and pottery. For example, adding cobalt oxide to glass produces a deep blue color.

Cobalt atoms

Cobalt itself is a metal, with a shiny, blue-silver appearance. Like other elements, atoms of cobalt are made up of three types of tiny particles: protons and neutrons in the nucleus (center) of each atom, and electrons orbiting the nucleus.

A proton has a positive charge. Neutrons have no charge at all—they are neutral. Electrons have a negative charge, which is equal and opposite to the charge of a proton. Opposites attract each other, so

Pure cobalt is rarely used on its own. Instead it is mixed with other metals to make useful alloys.

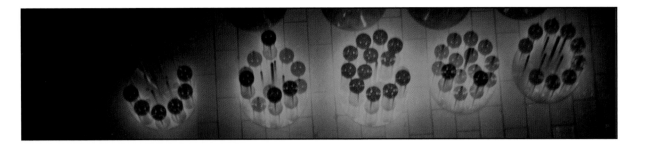

Tubes of radioactive cobalt-60 glow in a tank of water. The light is produced as cobalt-60 atoms break down into smaller, more stable atoms.

the electrons are pulled toward the protons. This is what keeps the atom together. The atomic number is the number of protons in an atom. Atoms have no overall charge so there is always the same number of electrons as protons in an atom. Cobalt's atomic number is 27, which means that all cobalt atoms have 27 protons and 27 electrons.

The total number of particles in the nucleus is called the atomic mass number. In nature, a cobalt atom has 27 protons plus 32 neutrons in its nucleus, making a total of 59 particles. However, there are many artificial cobalt isotopes. Isotopes are atoms with different numbers of neutrons. All of the artificial isotopes are radioactive, which means they break up and release radiation. The longest-lived of these is cobalt-60, which has a half-life of about 5 years. (The half-life is the time it takes for half of the atoms to break up into smaller atoms). Cobalt-60 is used as a source of radiation.

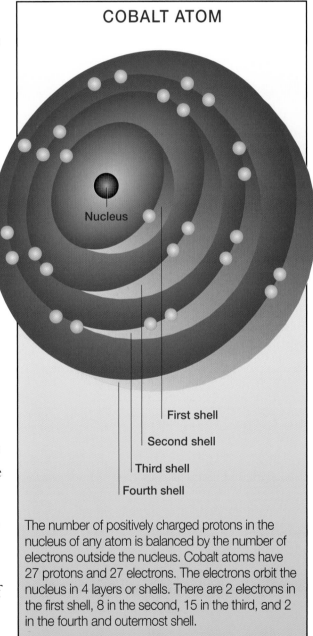

COBALT ATOM

Nucleus

First shell

Second shell

Third shell

Fourth shell

The number of positively charged protons in the nucleus of any atom is balanced by the number of electrons outside the nucleus. Cobalt atoms have 27 protons and 27 electrons. The electrons orbit the nucleus in 4 layers or shells. There are 2 electrons in the first shell, 8 in the second, 15 in the third, and 2 in the fourth and outermost shell.

Special characteristics

Perhaps the most unusual characteristic of the element cobalt is its ability to act as a magnet. This ability, called ferromagnetism, is possessed by only three elements—the metals iron, nickel, and cobalt.

While cobalt's magnetism is not as strong as that of iron, a magnetized piece of cobalt will stay magnetic up to a temperature of around 2012 °F (1100 °C). That is higher than any other element. Cobalt is combined with iron and nickel to make the best permanent magnets, which keep their magnetic strength for a long time.

Hard metal

As a solid, cobalt is a typical metal and is very similar to iron. It is hard—even a little bit harder than iron—and shiny, with high melting and boiling points. Like other metals, cobalt can conduct heat and electricity well.

Cobalt metal has two allotropes—solid forms in which the atoms are arranged in slightly different ways. This is similar to the way that the element carbon can exist as both the hard gemstone diamond and as soft graphite, which is used in pencil lead. The cobalt allotropes are much more similar to each other than those of carbon,

These lumps of cobalt are very old and are covered in dark oxide. Blue tinges on the surface show where the metal has formed compounds with other elements.

and they are usually found mixed up in a piece of cobalt. In one allotrope, which makes up most cobalt metal at temperatures below 782 °F (417 °C), the atoms are very closely packed together. In the other allotrope, which occurs mostly above that temperature, the atoms are a little more spread out.

Transition element

Cobalt's place in the periodic table is between iron and nickel in the middle section of the table. Because this section stretches across the periodic table, elements here are called transition elements (from the Latin word *trans*, meaning "across").

When elements react, the atoms of two or more elements join together to make a compound. The way an element reacts

Like other transition metals, cobalt is able to form compounds that have many different colors. The cobalt chloride here is purple. The color of the compounds depends on their crystal structure.

COBALT FACTS	
● Chemical symbol	Co
● Atomic number	27
● Atomic mass number	59
● Melting point	2723 °F (1495 °C)
● Boiling point	5252 °F (2900 °C)
● Density	8.9 grams per cubic cm (8.9 times that of water)

depends on how the electrons are arranged in its atoms. The atoms of cobalt and the other transition elements fill their electron shells in an unusual way. They all have inner electron shells that are not full. The unfilled shells make transition elements react in the same way. Like other transition elements, cobalt has several different oxidation states and can combine with other elements in many different ways.

Iron (II) sulphate

Chromium (III) sulphate

Cobalt chloride

Copper (II) sulphate

Nickel Sulphate

Potassium hexacyanoferrate (III)

DID YOU KNOW?

OXIDATION NUMBERS

Chemists use the term *oxidation state* to describe the way that elements join together to make compounds. As they react, many atoms lose or gain electrons and then become ions.

Atoms that lose electrons become positively charged ions. This is because there are now more positively charged protons than negatively charged electrons. Atoms that gain electrons take them from an atom that has lost electrons. These atoms become negative ions, with more electrons than protons. The ions with opposite charges are attracted to each other, forming a compound.

The oxidation number shows the amount of charge that an atom gains or loses as it forms a compound. Sodium, for example, has an oxidation number of +1 when it combines with chlorine. It loses an electron to the chlorine, becoming a sodium ion with a single positive charge. Many elements always have the same oxidation state. Cobalt, however, can have oxidation states of +1, +2, +3, or even +4. This variation is because of cobalt's unfilled inner electron shell, which can lose different numbers of electrons. Oxidation numbers are often written as Roman numbers in a compound's name.

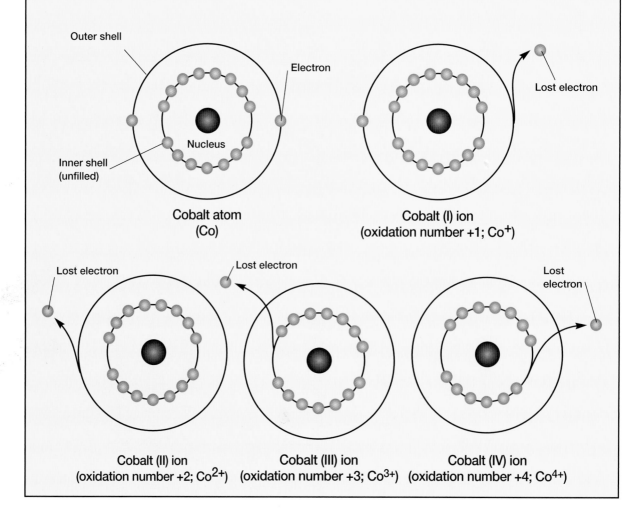

Outer shell
Electron
Nucleus
Inner shell (unfilled)

Cobalt atom
(Co)

Lost electron

Cobalt (I) ion
(oxidation number +1; Co^+)

Lost electron

Cobalt (II) ion
(oxidation number +2; Co^{2+})

Lost electron

Cobalt (III) ion
(oxidation number +3; Co^{3+})

Lost electron

Cobalt (IV) ion
(oxidation number +4; Co^{4+})

Cobalt in history

The element cobalt was not discovered until about two hundred years ago. However, the Egyptians and Persians of 2,000 years ago were using cobalt-containing substances to color their glass and pottery deep blue.

Spirited metal

The name *cobalt* tells the story of how cobalt was discovered. Several centuries ago, mountains in Germany were mined for minerals containing silver. When the miners tried to extract the silver, they often had problems and would say that naughty spirits or goblins were the cause.

They started calling troublesome ores Kobold, which is the German word for "goblin." Kobold ores produced no silver, just plenty of poisonous fumes. It was discovered later that these ores contained a substance that would give glass a deep blue color.

New element

Eventually, in 1739, the Swedish chemist Georg Brandt (1694–1768) showed that it was the presence of a previously unknown metal that was causing the blue color. Brandt named the metal cobalt rex (meaning "king goblin"). Cobalt was proven to be a single element in 1780.

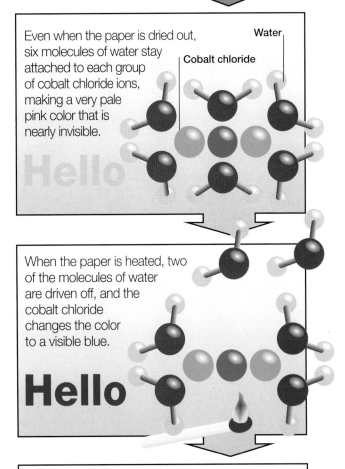

ATOMS AT WORK

The changing colors of one cobalt compound, cobalt chloride ($CoCl_2$), make it a good invisible ink. When cobalt chloride is dissolved in cold water it makes a pale pink liquid that can be used to write on paper. The pink writing is almost invisible until the paper is heated. This makes the cobalt chloride blue and reveals the message.

Chlorine ion

Pink solution

Cobalt ion

Even when the paper is dried out, six molecules of water stay attached to each group of cobalt chloride ions, making a very pale pink color that is nearly invisible.

Water

Cobalt chloride

When the paper is heated, two of the molecules of water are driven off, and the cobalt chloride changes the color to a visible blue.

Hello

The reaction that takes place can be written like this:

$$CoCl_2.6H_2O \rightarrow CoCl_2.4H_2O + 2H_2O$$

A period is used to show that the water (H_2O) is inside the crystal but not part of the compound.

Cobalt in nature

Unlike gold or platinum, cobalt is not a rare and precious metal. However, it does not exist in very large quantities in the Earth's crust.

Hard to find

Cobalt makes up only about 0.0025 percent of the Earth's crust, or one atom in every 40,000. Soil contains the most cobalt (about 0.005 percent), while seawater contains the least (0.00007 percent). Overall, cobalt is the thirty-third most common element on Earth.

Even where cobalt is mined, the concentrations in the rocks are often very low. It is usually only worth extracting the cobalt if another useful metal is also present in the rocks. However, because cobalt has so many uses, more cobalt ore is now being mined and pure metal produced.

Minerals

Cobalt is not found in nature in its pure form. Like most metals, it occurs as a variety

DID YOU KNOW?

COBALT IN THE COSMOS

Cobalt is very rare in the universe. For every one billion atoms in the universe, only 60 of them are cobalt. However, in the human body cobalt is even rarer. There are only two cobalt atoms out of every billion, even though it is essential for health. One of the most concentrated natural sources of cobalt is in meteorites—lumps of rock that land on Earth from space. On average, one billion atoms from a meteorite would contain 200,000 cobalt atoms. That is twenty times more cobalt than in the rocks on Earth.

These pink crystals are cobaltocalcite, a mineral containing cobalt carbonate ($CoCO_3$).

Like other cobalt minerals, these crystals of cobalt chloride have water molecules locked inside them. The amount of water in the crystal affects its color.

COBALT MINERALS

Name	Formula
Asbolite	$CoO_2.MnO_2.4H_2O$
Carrolite	$CuCo_2S_4$
Cobaltite	$CoAsS$
Erythrite	$3CoO.As_2O_5.8H_2O$
Heterogenite	$CoO.2Co_2O_3.6H_2O$
Linnaeite	Co_3S_4
Safflorite	$CoAs_2$
Skudderite	$CoAs_3$
Smaltite	$CoAs_2$
Sphaerocobaltite	$CoCO_2$

of different minerals. Many of these minerals contain other elements, especially arsenic and sulfur.

At present, there is no shortage of cobalt, but this may change in the next century. By then, people may need to search under the sea for cobalt. Although seawater itself contains very little cobalt, there are rich sources on the seabed that could eventually produce millions of tons of cobalt. Nodules containing cobalt and other metals (particularly manganese) are found deep underwater. Cobalt-rich rocks are also found at shallower depths, on the sides of underwater volcanoes.

Mining and refining

Every year, about 55,000 tons (50,000 tonnes) of cobalt are produced around the world. The largest sources of cobalt minerals are in Africa, particularly in the Democratic Republic of Congo (formerly called Zaire) and Zambia. Together, these two countries produce about half of the world's cobalt.

Starting point

There are many different starting points for making cobalt. This is because many different ores are used. Often, the ores used to produce cobalt are mined because they

This cobalt-containing ore is from a mine in the Democratic Republic of Congo. Often cobalt is not the most common metal in an ore.

contain useful amounts of copper, nickel, or lead. Cobalt is produced as an extra product in the refining process.

Even if a cobalt-only ore is used, the cobalt is chemically combined with other elements—usually arsenic, sulfur, and oxygen. The cobalt needs to be separated from these to make pure cobalt metal.

DID YOU KNOW?

COBALT PRICES

Precious metals such as gold and platinum are not the only metals with rapidly changing prices. At the end of 2003, the price of pure cobalt was $6.70 per pound, the lowest price for almost twenty years.

One year later, the price had rocketed to $22.00 per pound. It was still rising and reached $28.50 a few weeks later. The reason for this sudden rise was that people thought that there was not enough cobalt around for all the things it was needed for. When something is in short supply, prices rise. Prices later fell again, when people realized that there was more cobalt available.

COBALT PRODUCTION

World cobalt production in 2004:

D.R. of Congo	12,125 tons	(11,000 tonnes)
Zambia	9,920 tons	(9,000 tonnes)
Australia	7,720 tons	(7,000 tonnes)
Canada	5,730 tons	(5,200 tonnes)
Russia	5,300 tons	(4,800 tonnes)
Cuba	3,750 tons	(3,400 tonnes)
New Caledonia	1,650 tons	(1,500 tonnes)
Brazil	1,410 tons	(1,300 tonnes)
Morocco	1,410 tons	(1,300 tonnes)
Other countries	2,650 tons	(2,400 tonnes)

Refinement process

Cobalt ores are roasted (heated in air) during the first step of the refinement process. This normally produces a mixture of metal oxides, and a number of different processes can be used to separate the useful compounds from the mixture. One of the most common processes involves adding sulfuric acid to the mixture. This produces a solution of cobalt sulfate, mixed with other metal sulfates. (A solution is a liquid with a compound dissolved in it.)

Adding sodium hypochlorite to this solution produces cobalt trihydroxide. This compound is insoluble (does not dissolve), so it comes out of the solution as a solid powder, which sinks to the bottom. The solid cobalt trihydroxide can then be separated from all the other substances in the mixture. It is finally converted to cobalt metal.

ATOMS AT WORK

Cobalt trihydroxide ($Co(OH)_3$) is produced as part of the process to make pure cobalt. First, the cobalt trihydroxide is heated, producing cobalt oxide, Co_2O_3 and water (H_2O).

Colbalt trihydroxide

Cobalt

Oxygen

Hydrogen

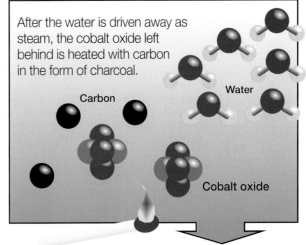

After the water is driven away as steam, the cobalt oxide left behind is heated with carbon in the form of charcoal.

Carbon

Water

Cobalt oxide

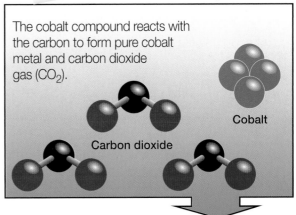

The cobalt compound reacts with the carbon to form pure cobalt metal and carbon dioxide gas (CO_2).

Carbon dioxide

Cobalt

The reactions that take place can be written like this:

$$2Co(OH)_3 \rightarrow Co_2O_3 + 3H_2O$$
$$2Co_2O_3 + 3C \rightarrow 4Co + 3CO_2$$

Cobalt chemistry

Cobalt is a transition element. Its chemistry is similar to other transition elements, such as manganese and iron. Although cobalt is not very reactive, it does form a large variety of compounds. It also has a remarkable ability to combine with several other atoms and molecules at the same time to form coordination compounds, which are also known as complexes.

Complexes are made when atoms or ions form bonds with a single central atom or ion. The surrounding objects are called ligands. Ligands are often small molecules, such as water (H_2O) or ammonia (NH_3). Complexes are held together by covalent bonds. These are bonds in which atoms share electrons, making both atoms more stable.

Donating electrons

Normal covalent bonds use two electrons—one from each of the atoms in the bond. For example, in a molecule of hydrogen gas (H_2), the bond is made from one electron from each of the hydrogen atoms. In a cobalt complex, however, both electrons used in the bond come from the ligand that is joined to a cobalt ion. These

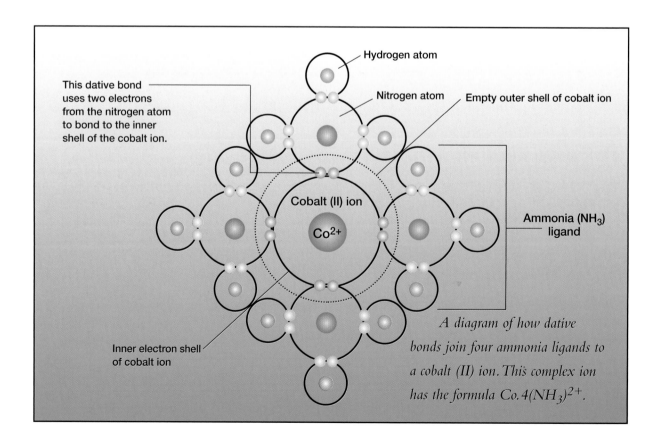

This dative bond uses two electrons from the nitrogen atom to bond to the inner shell of the cobalt ion.

Hydrogen atom

Nitrogen atom

Empty outer shell of cobalt ion

Cobalt (II) ion

Co^{2+}

Ammonia (NH_3) ligand

Inner electron shell of cobalt ion

A diagram of how dative bonds join four ammonia ligands to a cobalt (II) ion. This complex ion has the formula Co.$4(NH_3)^{2+}$.

sort of bonds are sometimes called dative bonds. This name comes from the Latin word *dativus*, which means "something that is given."

Cobalt complexes

All transition elements form complexes. The only element that forms more complexes than cobalt is platinum. The reason why cobalt and other transition elements are so good at forming complexes is because they have empty spaces in their inner electron shells.

The ligands that bond to the cobalt generally have a pair of electrons that is not involved in another bond. This pair has a small negative charge and it is attracted to the cobalt ion. (Elements such as nitrogen and oxygen have electron pairs and they are often found in ligands).

Most cobalt ions have lost either two (Co^{2+}) or three (Co^{3+}) of their electrons, so they have a strong positive charge. The ions are also slightly smaller than cobalt atoms because they have lost the outer shell of electrons. This makes the ions' positive charges even stronger.

The ligand's electron pair takes up places in the cobalt's unfilled inner electron shell. Cobalt (III) ions always have six ligands attached to them, so these compounds have a coordination number of six. Cobalt (II) ions have a coordination number of four.

Three solutions of cobalt ions in test tubes. The red solution on the left contains a complex of cobalt and six water molecules. When hydrochloric acid is added, the complex changes to one containing chloride ions, and the solution becomes blue (center). Adding more water reverses the reaction, and the solution becomes red again (right).

DISCOVERERS

ALFRED WERNER

The chemistry of coordination compounds was figured out in about 1900 by Alfred Werner (1866–1919), a Swiss chemist. His discoveries came from studying the chemistry of a variety of compounds, including compounds formed by cobalt (III) chloride with ammonia (NH_3). In 1913, Werner received science's top award, the Nobel Prize for Chemistry, for his discoveries.

Scientists already knew that complex compounds of ammonium cobalt chloride with the formulas $CoCl_3.6NH_3$, $CoCl_3.5NH_3$, and $CoCl_3.4NH_3$ existed. (The "." is used to show which part of the formula is the ligand. The first complex contained six ammonia ligands, the second had five, and the third had just four.) However, nobody understood how the chloride ions and ammonia were all bonded to the single cobalt ion in these different complexes.

To find out, Werner reacted each of these compounds with silver nitrate ($AgNO_3$) solution. Any chloride ions that were free and not bonded to the cobalt would react to form solid silver chloride. When $CoCl_3.6NH_3$ was used, three times the amount of silver chloride was produced than when $CoCl_3.4NH_3$ was reacted. Werner realized that this was because, in $CoCl_3.6NH_3$, all the chlorides are free ions dissolved in the water. In $CoCl_3.4NH_3$, however, only one chloride is a free ion. The other two are bonded to cobalt as ligands.

Werner had discovered that, in all these cobalt complexes, there were always six ligands bonded to the cobalt (III) ion. Some of these were chlorides ions, some were ammonia molecules. Werner introduced the term coordination number to describe the number of groups that are bonded to the central atom or ion.

This complex compound has the formula $CoCl_3.6NH_3$. It has a central cobalt ion (Co^{3+}). This is surrounded by six ammonia ligands (NH_3). When it is dissolved in water, there are also three chloride ions (Cl^-) floating freely. This complex makes a yellow solution.

Chloride ion

Cobalt ion

Dative bond

Nitrogen

Hydrogen

Ammonia (NH₃)

This complex compound has the formula $CoCl_3.4NH_3$. It has a central cobalt ion (Co^{3+}). This is surrounded by four ammonia ligands (NH_3). There are also two chloride ions (Cl^-) attached to the cobalt. When it is dissolved in water, there is just one chloride ion floating freely. This complex makes a green solution.

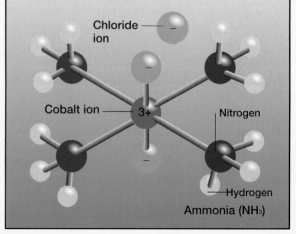

Chloride ion

Cobalt ion

Nitrogen

Hydrogen

Ammonia (NH₃)

Cobalt compounds

Like many other transition elements, cobalt forms compounds using different oxidation states. The most common oxidation states are +2 and +3. Compounds containing cobalt II (Co^{+2}) ions are called cobaltous. The compounds of cobalt III (Co^{+3}) ions are cobaltic.

Cobalt compounds are held together mainly by ionic bonds. These bonds form when ions with opposite charges are attracted to each other. All cobalt compounds need to be handled with care, because too much cobalt is poisonous.

Stable and unstable

Cobalt (II) compounds include those formed with the reactive gases called halogens—fluorine (CoF_2), chlorine ($CoCl_2$), bromine ($CoBr_2$), and iodine (CoI_2). Halogen compounds are generally stable. Cobalt (II) carbonate ($CoCO_3$) is also very stable. However, cobalt (II) hydroxide, $Co(OH)_2$, gradually changes in air to cobalt (III) hydroxide, $Co(OH)_3$.

Blue cobalt hydroxide powder forms inside a test tube and sinks to the bottom. This reaction occurs when sodium hydroxide (NaOH) is added to a solution. Chemists use this as a test for dissolved metal ions. They can usually identify which metal is present by the color of the powder that is produced.

17

ATOMS AT WORK

Cobalt metal reacts with sulfuric acid to form a sulfate compound. When added to water, the acid becomes hydrogen and sulfate ions.

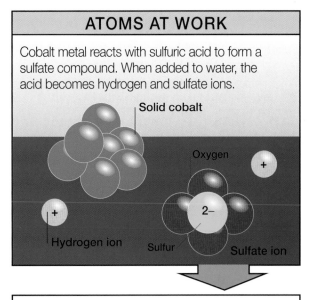

Solid cobalt

Oxygen

+

2−

+

Hydrogen ion

Sulfur

Sulfate ion

Each cobalt atom loses two electrons and becomes an ion. These are collected by the hydrogen ions, which become hydrogen atoms.

Cobalt

Electron

Hydrogen

2−

The hydrogen atoms form hydrogen gas molecules (H_2) and bubble away. The cobalt and sulfate ions left behind make a solution of cobalt sulfate.

Hydrogen gas

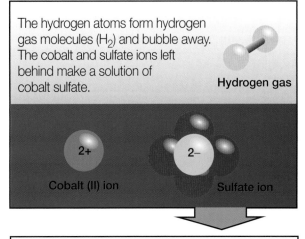

2+

2−

Cobalt (II) ion

Sulfate ion

The reactions that take place can be written like this:

$$Co + H_2SO_4 \rightarrow CoSO_4 + H_2$$

DID YOU KNOW?

Lumps of cobalt metal do not react with the air at normal temperatures. However, if the metal is ground to a fine powder, it becomes so reactive that it can burst into flames. The metal reacts with oxygen in the air, forming cobalt oxide. In large lumps there is not enough metal in contact with the air for a reaction. However, as a fine powder, the area of metal exposed to the air is much greater, so the reaction can take place.

Most simple cobalt (III) compounds with halogens are unstable, except when molecules of ammonia are added to form complex compounds. The exception is cobalt (III) fluoride, CoF_3. This is a brown powder used to add fluorine atoms to carbon compounds to make very stable and unreactive gases called fluorocarbons. Cobalt (II) nitrate, $Co(NO_3)_2$, is also stable. Cobalt (III) nitrate is not, except when ammonia (or a similar ligand) is added to the molecule.

Oxides

Cobalt forms three main oxides. Cobalt (III) oxide, Co_2O_3, is a black compound formed when cobalt metal is heated slightly in plenty of air. At temperatures of 750 to 1560 °F (400 to 850 °C), Co_3O_4 is produced. Above 2010 °F (1100 °C) cobalt (II) oxide, or cobalt monoxide (CoO) forms. The cobalt oxide used in industry contains a mixture of these compounds.

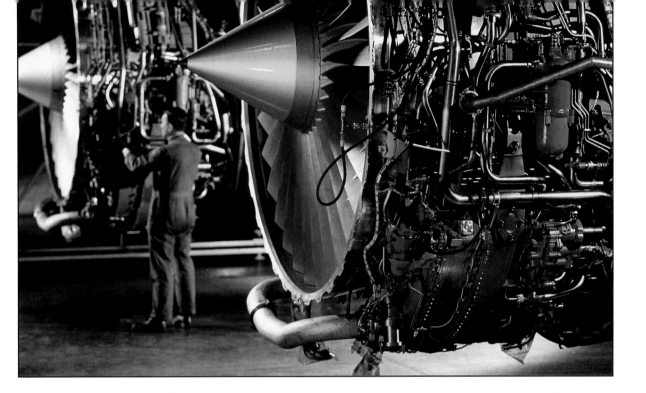

Uses of cobalt

Cobalt is an ingredient in the tough alloys used to make the fan blades inside jet engines.

Unlike metallic elements such as iron and copper, cobalt is rarely used on its own to make things. However, cobalt has a huge number of uses, because when it is added to a material it can make important differences in that material's properties.

Superalloys

The most common use of cobalt is in making alloys, or mixtures of metals. Cobalt is usually mixed with iron and nickel, plus some other elements, such as tungsten and manganese. These "superalloys" can stand up to high forces and very high temperatures—up to about 1800 °F (980 °C). They do not corrode (rust or decay), and can act like a super-tough stainless steel. Cobalt superalloys were originally developed for the turbines (fans) in jet engines. They are now used to make many other things, including nuclear reactors and spacecraft.

Cobalt is also used to make alloys that are extremely hard and can stand up to huge amounts of wear and tear. For example, some artificial hip and knee joints are made from an alloy containing cobalt, chromium, and tungsten.

Cobalt alloys that do not change shape as they heat up and cool down have also been developed. These are used in measuring instruments where high accuracy is needed at high temperatures.

COBALT FACTS	
HOW COBALT IS USED	
Superalloys and other hard alloys	25.5%
Batteries	21.0%
Colors	11.0%
Catalysts	11.0%
Hard materials	10.5%
Paint driers and adhesives	9.5%
Magnets	7.0%
Electrical/electronic	4.5%

Tungsten carbide is a material used when a very hard cutting edge is needed, such as in industrial drills. The material used to make tungsten carbide tools contains cobalt as a binder. The cobalt makes the tools tough, shock-resistant and hard. Cobalt also acts as a binder in making tools that use industrial diamonds, such as certain types of saws.

Batteries

A lot of cobalt is used to make mobile phones and laptop computers. This is because cobalt is an essential element in the two main types of modern rechargeable batteries.

Magnets

The magnetic nature of cobalt has led to its use in strong, long-lasting magnets. These are magnetized by placing them in a strong magnetic field. Hard magnets are made from alnico alloy, which contains aluminum, nickel, and cobalt.

A more familiar use for cobalt's magnetic properties is in recording tape. This is used in video and music cassettes. Generally the tape is rolled up inside a cassette and is passed through a playing device. Recording tape works by having an electric signal turn a magnetic coating

on the tape into a fixed pattern. The player then reads this pattern and plays back the recorded sound or picture. The magnetic layer is made of iron oxide particles with a little cobalt mixed in.

Chemicals

Cobalt is also a useful catalyst. A catalyst is a substance that helps a chemical reaction take place. (The catalyst is not changed in any way.) Small hydrocarbon gas molecules (made from carbon and hydrogen), such as natural gas, or methane (CH_4), are turned into larger, liquid molecules using a cobalt catalyst. These liquid hydrocarbons are easier to transport than natural gas, and can be used in place of certain fuels.

Oil refineries make useful chemicals from petroleum. Cobalt is an important catalyst in this process.

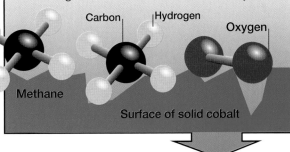

ATOMS AT WORK

Cobalt is used as the catalyst in the reaction that converts methane gas (CH_4) into larger molecules. Two methanes and an oxygen molecule (O_2) from the air cling to the surface of the cobalt catalyst.

Carbon · Hydrogen · Oxygen

Methane

Surface of solid cobalt

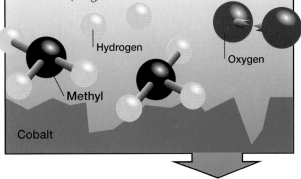

The oxygen molecule separates into two atoms, and one hydrogen atom is lost from each of the methane molecules, making methyl molecules (CH_3).

Hydrogen

Oxygen

Methyl

Cobalt

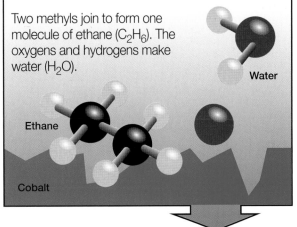

Two methyls join to form one molecule of ethane (C_2H_6). The oxygens and hydrogens make water (H_2O).

Water

Ethane

Cobalt

The reaction that takes place can be written like this:
$$4CH_4 + O_2 \rightarrow 2C_2H_6 + 2H_2O$$

Coloring with cobalt

Many people have heard of cobalt because of vivid cobalt blue color used in glass and to make paints. In fact, cobalt compounds can produce a variety of other colors, but it is these rich blues that are most associated with cobalt.

Coloring glass

The use of cobalt oxide to color glass dates back to ancient times. A piece of blue cobalt glass was found in the tomb of the ancient Egyptian pharaoh Tutankhamen, who died more than 4,300 years ago.

Cobalt is used to make blue glass. Blue glass bottle and jugs were once highly prized. Today, other compounds are used to make colored glass.

Glass colored with cobalt is often called Bristol blue glass because large quantities were made in the city of Bristol, England, since about 1650.

Cobalt oxide is also used in very small amounts (about two atoms in every million, or 2 grams in every tonne of glass)

COBALT FACTS

COBALT COLORS
Cobalt oxide is mixed with other compounds to produce a variety of different colors:

Color	Added ingredient
Blue	aluminum oxide
Purple-blue	silicon and potassium oxides
Violet	phosphorus oxide
Light blue	selenium and silicon oxides
Turquoise	chromium and aluminum oxides
Green	zinc oxide
Pink	magnesium oxide
Brown	iron oxide
Gray-black	no added ingredient

SEE FOR YOURSELF

THE WORLD IN BLUE

Find an object made of blue-colored glass or plastic and try looking through it. How does it change the color of the objects you see? You will probably find that most blue things still look blue, but red things look much darker, and yellow objects become muddy looking. This is because more blue rays of light pass through the glass than any other color, so while blue objects look the same, things with another color look darker or duller than normal.

to make colorless glass. The slight gray-blue color produced by the cobalt oxide counteracts the yellowing caused by iron impurities in the glass.

Pottery

Cobalt compounds are used to decorate fine pottery. Cobalt oxide—alone or mixed with other compounds—is painted on the clay, and the glaze (protective covering) is added on top. When the item is heated to harden it, the cobalt oxide may react with other compounds in the paint, producing the strong color. Many traditional pottery styles have made use of cobalt colors. Most famously, cobalt was used to make the classic blue designs on Chinese porcelain from as far back as about 1300 C.E. Later, European china was being colored with cobalt, including Dutch Delft pottery and British Spode.

Painters have also made use of cobalt oxide. Discovered in 1802, the cobalt blue pigment, which was cobalt oxide with aluminum oxide, colored oil paints and was used by artists such as Claude Monet. Cerulean blue, a slightly paler color, was invented in 1860 and used by painters mostly for depicting clear skies. Both colors are still in use today.

Traditional Chinese porcelain is painted with a cobalt-containing blue dye before being fired. This type of pottery is named china for the country where it was invented.

Cobalt and health

A n adult human's body contains about 3 milligrams of cobalt. This is not as pure metal, but in vitamin B_{12}, which is also called cobalamin. Each molecule of this vital substance contains an atom of cobalt at its center.

Vital compound

Vitamin B_{12} works with other substances in the body to carry out life processes, including producing red blood cells and DNA, which is the molecule that holds important genetic material. It also helps the nervous system to work properly. The most serious effect of not having enough vitamin B_{12} in the body is a disease called pernicious anemia. People with this disease are unable to absorb vitamin B_{12} and have unusual red blood cells and damaged nerves. This disease used to be fatal but can now be treated.

Because the human body cannot make vitamin B_{12}, people have to get it from their food. Most of us eat about 57 micrograms of vitamin B_{12} each day, which is more than enough. Vitamin B_{12} is produced by bacteria in soil and in the stomachs of animals, such as cows. It is found in meat and dairy products, but not in most plants. Non-dairy vegetarians may have to take B_{12} supplements.

Cobalt is the essential ingredient of vitamin B_{12}. This vitamin is found in foods made from animal products, such as cheese.

A STRANGE EXPERIMENT

By the 1920s, it was known that people with the serious illness pernicious anemia could be cured by eating raw liver. However, doctors did not know why this treatment worked, and why cooked meats were not so effective.

In 1928, William Castle, a doctor at Harvard University, did an experiment to find out why. First, he ate some red meat, then he made himself vomit and fed the vomited meat to his patients. Castle found that this diet worked as well as liver. He realized that there was something in his stomach juices that the patients needed.

In 1948, scientists discovered that vitamin B_{12} was the vital ingredient in liver and red meat, and that the stomach juices enabled the body to absorb vitamin B_{12}. Though it was dangerous—and should not be repeated—Castle's experiment saved thousands of lives.

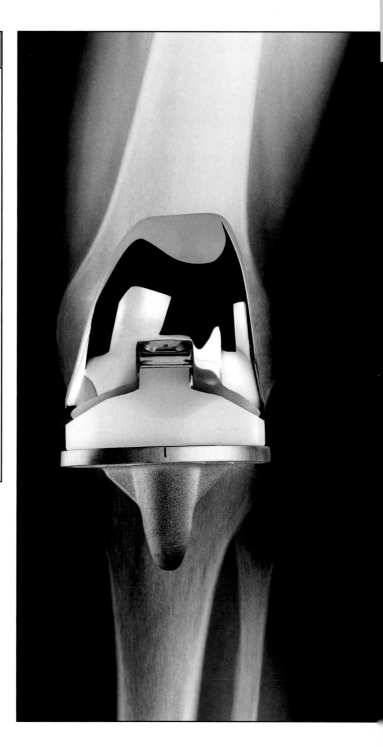

Cancer treatment

There are other ways in which cobalt is important for health. People with cancer often receive radiation treatment to kill the cancer. This radiation usually comes from the radioactive isotope cobalt-60. The radiation is focused into a beam so it can pass into the body and kill only the cancer cells inside.

Radiation from cobalt-60 is also used as a sterilizing, or cleaning, process. This is useful for sensitive instruments and tools that would be damaged by heat during sterilization.

Cobalt is one of the metals used to make artificial joints, such as this knee. Artificial joints are fitted to the ends of bones that have worn down. The cobalt makes the new joint very tough and durable.

Cobalt in the environment

Clover absorbs cobalt compounds from the soil.

Most of the cobalt found in the environment is from natural sources. Cobalt from rocks enters water and lakes as the rocks wear away through a natural process called erosion. From there, the cobalt enters the sea and the soil. Microscopic life-forms, such as bacteria, in the roots of certain plants, can take cobalt from the soil and pass it to the growing plant. Grazing animals, such as cattle and sheep, then eat these plants. The cobalt is absorbed into the blood and used by the animal's body.

Coal also contains cobalt, so small amounts of cobalt compounds enter the air through burning coal in power stations. Other industrial uses of cobalt, such as glassmaking, also release some cobalt into the environment.

The way cobalt is constantly being deposited in soils and taken into plants is called the cobalt cycle. Each year, 55,000 tons (50,000 tonnes) of cobalt enter the air, rivers, and living things. About 20 percent comes from human activity, while 80 percent comes from natural processes.

Too little and too much

A small amount of cobalt is needed for good health. Grazing animals become ill if the cobalt concentration in soils is too low.

In general, when small amounts are handled properly, cobalt is not poisonous. However, people who work with cobalt

DID YOU KNOW?

COBALT IN BEER

During the 1970s, a Canadian beer manufacturer added tiny amounts of cobalt compounds to beer to prevent the bubbles from bursting too quickly. Unfortunately, these additives became a serious source of cobalt poisoning for people who were addicted to drinking beer. Those who drank more than eight bottles of beer a day sometimes suffered damage to their heart because of the added cobalt, and some died because of this.

and its compounds have to be careful, because cobalt can be harmful in high doses or if breathed in. It can cause lung diseases and cancers and damage the skin and heart. For this reason, there are strict limits on how much cobalt is allowed in a worker's environment. In the United States, this limit is 0.1 milligrams per cubic meter of air. In some other countries the limit is five times lower (0.02 milligrams per cubic meter) to keep health risks to a minimum.

Cobalt chloride is used in humidity detectors that tell people how much moisture is in the air. When the air is dry, the crystals are a pale purple (left). When the air becomes more humid (moist) the crystals become much darker as they absorb water from the air.

Periodic table

Everything in the universe is made from combinations of substances called elements. Elements are made of tiny atoms, which are too small to see. Atoms are the building blocks of all matter.

The character of an atom depends on how many protons there are in its center, or nucleus. An element's atomic number is the same as the number of its protons. An atom has the same number of electrons as protons.

Scientists have found around 116 different elements. About 90 elements occur naturally on Earth. The rest have been made in experiments.

All these elements are set out on a chart called the periodic table. This lists all the elements in order according to their atomic number.

The elements at the left of the table are metals. Those at the right are nonmetals. Between the metals and the nonmetals are the metalloids, which sometimes act like metals and sometimes like nonmetals.

● On the left of the table are the alkali metals. These have just one outer electron.

● Metals get more reactive as you go down a group. The most reactive nonmetals are at the top of the table.

● On the right of the periodic table are the noble gases. These elements have full outer shells.

● The number of electrons orbiting the nucleus increases down each group.

● Elements in the same group have the same number of electrons in their outer shells.

● The transition metals are in the middle of the table, between Groups II and III.

Group I

Group II

Transition metals

Group I	Group II							
1 H Hydrogen 1								
3 Li Lithium 7	4 Be Beryllium 9							
11 Na Sodium 23	12 Mg Magnesium 24							
19 K Potassium 39	20 Ca Calcium 40	21 Sc Scandium 45	22 Ti Titanium 48	23 V Vanadium 51	24 Cr Chromium 52	25 Mn Manganese 55	26 Fe Iron 56	27 Co Cobalt 59
37 Rb Rubidium 85	38 Sr Strontium 88	39 Y Yttrium 89	40 Zr Zirconium 91	41 Nb Niobium 93	42 Mo Molybdenum 96	43 Tc Technetium (98)	44 Ru Ruthenium 101	45 Rh Rhodium 103
55 Cs Cesium 133	56 Ba Barium 137	71 Lu Lutetium 175	72 Hf Hafnium 179	73 Ta Tantalum 181	74 W Tungsten 184	75 Re Rhenium 186	76 Os Osmium 190	77 Ir Iridium 192
87 Fr Francium 223	88 Ra Radium 226	103 Lr Lawrencium (260)	104 Rf Rutherfordium (263)	105 Db Dubnium (268)	106 Sg Seaborgium (266)	107 Bh Bohrium (272)	108 Hs Hassium (277)	109 Mt Meitnerium (276)

Lanthanide elements

Actinide elements

57 La Lanthanum 39	58 Ce Cerium 140	59 Pr Praseodymium 141	60 Nd Neodymium 144	61 Pm Promethium (145)
89 Ac Actinium 227	90 Th Thorium 232	91 Pa Protactinium 231	92 U Uranium 238	93 Np Neptunium (237)

The horizontal rows are called periods. As you go across a period, the atomic number increases by one from each element to the next. The vertical columns are called groups. Elements get heavier as you go down a group. All the elements in a group have the same number of electrons in their outer shells. This means they react in similar ways.

The transition metals fall between Groups II and III. Their electron shells fill up in an unusual way. The lanthanide elements and the actinide elements are set apart from the main table to make it easier to read. All the lanthanide elements and the actinide elements are quite rare.

Cobalt in the table

Cobalt is in the first period of the transition metals. Like other transition metals, cobalt atoms have empty spaces in their two outermost electron shells. This allows them to form large compounds called complexes. Cobalt complexes have several atoms or small molecules, called ligands, attached to a central cobalt ion.

Metals

Metalloids (semimetals)

Nonmetals

27
Co
Cobalt
59

Atomic (proton) number
Symbol
Name
Atomic mass

Group VIII

Group III	Group IV	Group V	Group VI	Group VII	Group VIII
					2 He Helium 4
5 B Boron 11	6 C Carbon 12	7 N Nitrogen 14	8 O Oxygen 16	9 F Fluorine 19	10 Ne Neon 20
13 Al Aluminum 27	14 Si Silicon 28	15 P Phosphorus 31	16 S Sulfur 32	17 Cl Chlorine 35	18 Ar Argon 40

28 Ni Nickel 59	29 Cu Copper 64	30 Zn Zinc 65	31 Ga Gallium 70	32 Ge Germanium 73	33 As Arsenic 75	34 Se Selenium 79	35 Br Bromine 80	36 Kr Krypton 84
46 Pd Palladium 106	47 Ag Silver 108	48 Cd Cadmium 112	49 In Indium 115	50 Sn Tin 119	51 Sb Antimony 122	52 Te Tellurium 128	53 I Iodine 127	54 Xe Xenon 131
78 Pt Platinum 195	79 Au Gold 197	80 Hg Mercury 201	81 Tl Thallium 204	82 Pb Lead 207	83 Bi Bismuth 209	84 Po Polonium (209)	85 At Astatine (210)	86 Rn Radon (222)
110 Ds Darmstadtium (281)	111 Rg Roentgenium (280)	112 Uub Ununbium (285)	113 Uut Ununtrium (284)	114 Uuq Ununquadium (289)	115 Uup Ununpentium (288)	116 Uuh Ununhexium (292)		

62 Sm Samarium 150	63 Eu Europium 152	64 Gd Gadolinium 157	65 Tb Terbium 159	66 Dy Dysprosium 163	67 Ho Holmium 165	68 Er Erbium 167	69 Tm Thulium 169	70 Yb Ytterbium 173
94 Pu Plutonium (244)	95 Am Americium (243)	96 Cm Curium (247)	97 Bk Berkelium (247)	98 Cf Californium (251)	99 Es Einsteinium (252)	100 Fm Fermium (257)	101 Md Mendelevium (258)	102 No Nobelium (259)

Chemical reactions

Chemical reactions are going on around us all the time. Some reactions involve just two substances, while others involve many more. But whenever a reaction takes place, at least one substance is changed.

In a chemical reaction, the number and type of atoms stay the same. But they join up in different combinations to form new molecules.

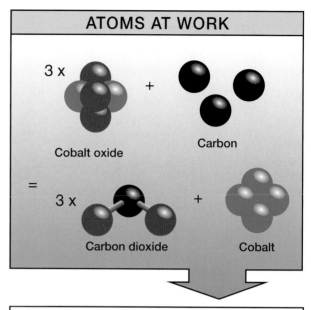

ATOMS AT WORK

$3 \times$ Cobalt oxide $+$ Carbon

$=$ $3 \times$ Carbon dioxide $+$ Cobalt

The reaction that takes place when cobalt oxide and carbon is written like this:

$$2Co_2O_3 + 3C \rightarrow 4Co + 3CO_2$$

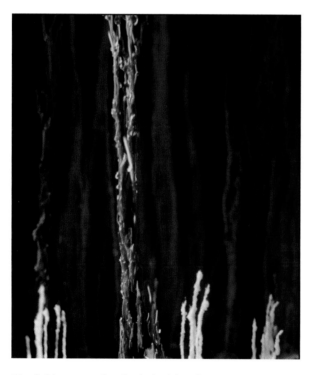

Dark blue crystals of cobalt chloride grow in a crystal garden. The ions used to make each crystal were originally dissolved in a solution. However, as the solution cools fewer ions can be dissolved in it, and the cobalt ions begin to form solid crystals.

Writing an equation

Chemical reactions can be described by writing down the atoms and molecules before and after the reaction. Since the atoms stay the same, the number of atoms before will be the same as the number of atoms after. Chemists write the reaction as an equation. This equation shows what happens during the chemical reaction.

Making it balance

When the numbers of each atom on both sides of the equation are equal, the equation is balanced. If the numbers are not equal, something is wrong. So the chemist adjusts the number of atoms involved until the equation is balanced.

Glossary

acid: An acid is a chemical that releases hydrogen ions easily during reactions.

atom: The smallest part of an element having all the properties of that element. Each atom is less than a millionth of an inch in diameter.

atomic mass number: The number of protons and neutrons in an atom.

atomic number: The number of protons in an atom.

bond: The attraction between two atoms, or ions, that holds them together.

compound: A substance made of atoms of two or more elements. The atoms are held together by chemical bonds.

corrosion: The eating away of a material by reaction with other chemicals, often oxygen and moisture in the air.

crystal: A solid consisting of a repeating pattern of atoms, ions, or molecules.

dissolve: A solid substance mixing with a liquid, or solvent, very evenly so that the solid disappears.

electron: A tiny particle with a negative charge. Inside atoms, electrons move around the nucleus in layers called shells.

element: A substance that is made from only one type of atom.

ion: An atom or a group of atoms that has lost or gained electrons to become electrically charged.

isotopes: Atoms of an element with the same number of protons and electrons but different numbers of neutrons.

mineral: A compound or element as it is found in its natural form in Earth.

metal: An element on the left-hand side of the periodic table.

molecule: A unit that contains atoms held together by chemical bonds.

nuclear reactor: A machine that controls a nuclear reaction happening inside it.

nucleus: The dense structure at the center of an atom. Protons and neutrons are found inside the nucleus of an atom.

neutron: A tiny particle with no electrical charge. Neutrons are found in the nucleus of almost every atom.

ore: A mineral that contains enough of a substance to make it useful for mining.

periodic table: A chart of all the chemical elements laid out in order of their atomic number.

proton: A tiny particle with a positive charge. Protons are found in the nucleus.

reaction: A process in which two or more elements or compounds combine to produce new substances.

solution: A liquid that has another substance dissolved in it.

transition metal: An element positioned in the middle of the periodic table. Transition metals, including cobalt, have spaces in their outer electron shell and in the next shell in.

Index